"9Marks, as a ministry, has taken basic biblical te  the hands of pastors. Bobby, by way of these stu delivered it to the person in the pew. I am unawa and practically helps Christians understand God's to use these studies in my own congregation."

 Jeramie Rinne, Senior Pastor, South Shore Baptist Church, Hingham, Massachusetts

"Bobby Jamieson has done local church pastors an incredible service by writing these study guides. Clear, biblical, and practical, they introduce the biblical basis for a healthy church. But more importantly, they challenge and equip church members to be part of the process of improving their own church's health. The studies work for individual, small group, and larger group settings. I have used them for the last year at my own church and appreciate how easy they are to adapt to my own setting. I don't know of anything else like them. Highly recommended!"

 Michael Lawrence, Senior Pastor, Hinson Baptist Church, *Biblical Theology in the Life of the Church*

"This is a Bible study that is actually rooted in the Bible and involves actual study. In the 9Marks Healthy Church Study Guides series a new standard has been set for personal theological discovery and corresponding personal application. Rich exposition, compelling questions, and clear syntheses combine to give a guided tour of ecclesiology—the theology of the church. I know of no better curriculum for generating understanding of and involvement in the church than this. It will be a welcome resource in our church for years to come."

 Rick Holland, Senior Pastor, Mission Road Bible Church, Prairie Village, Kansas

"In America today we have the largest churches in the history of our nation, but the least amount of impact for Christ's kingdom. Slick marketing and finely polished vision statements are a foundation of sand. The 9Marks Healthy Church Study Guides series is a refreshing departure from church-growth materials, towards an in-depth study of God's Word that will equip God's people with his vision for his Church. These study guides will lead local congregations to abandon secular methodologies for church growth and instead rely on Christ's principles for developing healthy, God-honoring assemblies."

 Carl J. Broggi, Senior Pastor, Community Bible Church, Beaufort, South Carolina; President, Search the Scriptures Radio Ministry

"Anyone who loves Jesus will love what Jesus loves. The Bible clearly teaches that Jesus loves the church. He knows about and cares for individual churches and wants them to be spiritually healthy and vibrant. Not only has Jesus laid down his life for the church but he has also given many instructions in his Word regarding how churches are to live and function in the world. This series of Bible studies by 9Marks shows how Scripture teaches these things. Any Christian who works through this curriculum, preferably with other believers, will be helped to see in fresh ways the wisdom, love, and power of God in establishing the church on earth. These studies are biblical, practical, and accessible. I highly recommend this curriculum as a useful tool that will help any church embrace its calling to display the glory of God to a watching world."

 Thomas Ascol, Senior Pastor, Grace Baptist Church of Cape Coral, Florida; Executive Director, Founders Ministries

9MARKS HEALTHY CHURCH STUDY GUIDES

Built upon the Rock: The Church

Hearing God's Word: Expositional Preaching

The Whole Truth about God: Biblical Theology

God's Good News: The Gospel

Real Change: Conversion

Reaching the Lost: Evangelism

Committing to One Another: Church Membership

Guarding One Another: Church Discipline

Growing One Another: Discipleship in the Church

Leading One Another: Church Leadership

THE WHOLE TRUTH ABOUT GOD: BIBLICAL THEOLOGY

Bobby Jamieson
Mark Dever, General Editor
Jonathan Leeman, Managing Editor

HEALTHY CHURCH STUDY GUIDES

CROSSWAY
WHEATON, ILLINOIS

The Whole Truth about God: Biblical Theology

Copyright © 2012 by 9Marks

Published by Crossway
          1300 Crescent Street
          Wheaton, Illinois 60187

Cover design: Dual Identity inc.

First printing 2012

Printed in the United States of America

Unless otherwise indicated, Scripture quotations are from the ESV® Bible (*The Holy Bible, English Standard Version*®), copyright © 2001 by Crossway. Used by permission. All rights reserved.

Scripture references marked NIV are taken from *The Holy Bible, New International Version*®, NIV®. Copyright © 1973, 1978, 1984, 2011 by Biblica, Inc.™ Used by permission. All rights reserved worldwide.

All emphases in Scripture have been added by the author.

Trade paperback ISBN: 978-1-4335-2532-2

PDF ISBN: 978-1-4335-2533-9

Mobipocket ISBN: 978-1-4335-2534-6

ePub ISBN: 978-1-4335-2535-3

Crossway is a publishing ministry of Good News Publishers.

LB		20	19	18	17	16	15	14	13	12
15	14	13	12	11	10	9	8	7	6	5	4	3	2	1

CONTENTS

INTRODUCTION

What does the local church mean to you?

Maybe you love your church. You love the people. You love the preaching and the singing. You can't wait to show up on Sunday, and you cherish fellowship with other church members throughout the week.

Then again, maybe your church is just a place you show up to a couple times a month. You sneak in late, duck out early.

We at 9Marks are convinced that the local church is where God means to display his glory to the nations. And we want to help you catch this vision, together with your whole church.

The 9Marks Healthy Church Study Guides are a series of six- or seven-week studies on each of the "nine marks of a healthy church" plus one introductory study. These nine marks are the core convictions of our ministry. To provide a quick introduction to them, we've included a chapter from Mark Dever's book *What Is a Healthy Church?* with each study. We don't claim that these nine marks are the most important things about the church or the only important things about the church. But we do believe that they are biblical and therefore helpful for churches.

So, in these studies, we're going to work through the biblical foundations and practical applications of each mark. The ten studies are:

- *Built upon the Rock: The Church* (the introductory study)
- *Hearing God's Word: Expositional Preaching*
- *The Whole Truth about God: Biblical Theology*
- *God's Good News: The Gospel*
- *Real Change: Conversion*
- *Reaching the Lost: Evangelism*
- *Committing to One Another: Church Membership*

- *Guarding One Another: Church Discipline*
- *Growing One Another: Discipleship in the Church*
- *Leading One Another: Church Leadership*

Each session of these studies takes a close look at one or more passages of Scripture and considers how to apply it to the life of your congregation. We hope they are equally appropriate for Sunday school, small groups, and other contexts where a group of two to two-hundred people can come together and discuss God's Word.

These studies are mainly driven by observation, interpretation, and application questions, so get ready to speak up! We also hope that these studies provide opportunities for people to reflect together on their experiences in the church, whatever those experiences may be.

God is a God of truth. He cannot tell a lie. He cannot deny himself. Every word of his proves true.

And God is a speaking God. He has spoken to us in his Word, revealing himself. He has revealed his holy character, his judgment against our sin, his glorious plan of salvation, and his certain promises for the future. And when God speaks, we must listen.

That's what theology is: listening to what God has said to us in his Word. And one of the most important things a church can do is get its theology right, because only a right theology can lead to a right worship and a right obedience. Every church should strive to believe and confess and live in light of a truly biblical theology.

In this study we're going to consider why biblical theology is important and then see how biblical theology fuels our churches' love, holiness, worship, witness, and unity. Let's listen carefully together to what God has said about why we must listen well to him.

AN ESSENTIAL MARK OF A HEALTHY CHURCH: BIBLICAL THEOLOGY

BY MARK DEVER

(Originally published as chapter 6 of What Is a Healthy Church?*)*

What do you think these italicized words mean: "But we know that when Christ appears, *we shall be like him*, for we shall see him as he is" (1 John 3:2 NIV).

If you carefully read through the biblical storyline presented in chapter 3, you would probably know that these words point to how, at the end of time, the church will purely reflect God's loving and holy character apart from the distorting influence of sin.

Yet if you were sitting in a Mormon tabernacle, you would hear that the words "we will be like him" mean that we will all become gods!

What's the difference between these two interpretations? One is informed by the theology of the whole Bible; the other is not.

I have argued in a number of places that expository preaching is essential for the health of a church. Yet every method of preaching, however good, is open to abuse. Our churches should not only be concerned with how we are taught, but also with what we are taught. That's why an essential mark of a healthy church is sound biblical theology, or theology that's biblical. Otherwise we will interpret individual verses to mean whatever we want them to mean.

SOUNDNESS

Soundness is an old-fashioned word. Yet we should cherish soundness—soundness in our understanding of the God of the Bible and his ways with us. Paul uses the word "sound" a number of times in his pastoral writings to Timothy and Titus. It means "reliable," "accurate," or "faithful." At root, it is an image from the medical world meaning whole or healthy. Biblically sound theology, then, is theology that is faithful to the teaching of the entire Bible. It reliably and accurately interprets the parts in terms of the whole.

In his first letter to Timothy, Paul says that "sound doctrine" is doctrine that "conforms to the gospel" and opposes ungodliness and sin (1 Tim. 1:10–11 NIV). Later on, he contrasts "false doctrines" with "the sound instruction of our Lord Jesus Christ and . . . godly teaching" (1 Tim. 6:3 NIV).

In his second letter to Timothy, Paul exhorts him, "What you heard from me, keep as the pattern of sound teaching, with faith and love in Christ Jesus" (2 Tim. 1:13 NIV). Then he warns Timothy that "the time will come when people will not put up with sound doctrine. Instead, to suit their own desires, they will gather around them a great number of teachers to say what their itching ears want to hear" (2 Tim. 4:3 NIV).

When Paul writes another young pastor, Titus, he shares similar concerns. Every man Titus appoints as an elder of a church, Paul says, "must hold firmly to the trustworthy message as it has been taught, so that he can encourage others by sound doctrine and refute those who oppose it" (Titus 1:9 NIV). False teachers must be rebuked "so that they will be sound in the faith" (Titus 1:13 NIV). And, finally, Titus "must teach what is appropriate to sound doctrine" (Titus 2:1 NIV).

Pastors should teach sound doctrine—doctrine that is reliable, accurate, and faithful to the Bible, and churches are responsible for keeping their pastors accountable to sound doctrine.

UNITY, DIVERSITY, AND CHARITY

We cannot lay out here everything that constitutes sound teaching since that would require us to reproduce the whole Bible. But in practice, every church decides where it requires complete agreement, where it permits limited disagreement, and where it allows complete liberty.

In the church I serve in Washington, DC, we require every member to believe in salvation through the work of Jesus Christ alone. We also confess the same (or very similar) understandings of believer's baptism and of church structure (that is, who has the final say in decisions). Agreement on baptism and structure are not essential for salvation, but they're practically helpful and health giving for the life of the church.

On the other hand, our church allows some disagreement over matters that are necessary neither for salvation nor for the practical life of the church. We all agree that Christ will return, but there is a range of opinions about the timing of his return.

Finally, our church allows entire liberty on matters still less central or clear, such as the rightness of armed resistance or the question of who wrote the book of Hebrews.

There's a principle running through all of this: the closer we get to the heart of our faith, the more we expect unity in our understanding of the faith—in sound biblical doctrine. The early church put it this way: in essentials, unity; in nonessentials, diversity; in all things, charity.

COMPLEX OR CONTROVERSIAL DOCTRINES

A church that is committed to sound teaching will commit to teaching the biblical doctrines churches too often neglect. To our eyes, certain doctrines may look difficult or even divisive. Yet we can trust that God has included them in his Word because they are foundational for understanding his work in salvation.

The Holy Spirit is no fool. If he has revealed something in his Book for all the world to read, churches should not think of themselves as so wise that they do better to avoid certain subjects. Should they exercise pastoral wisdom and care when speaking about some things? Surely. Should they avoid those things entirely? Surely not. If we want churches that are guided by sound doctrine from the Bible, we must come to terms with the entire Bible.

The biblical doctrine of election, for example, is often avoided as too complex or too confusing. Be that as it may, the doctrine is undeniably biblical. While we may not understand everything about election, it is no small matter that our salvation ultimately issues from God rather than from ourselves. There are a number of important questions that the Bible answers but churches commonly neglect such as:

- Are people basically bad or good? Do they merely need encouragement and self-esteem, or do they need forgiveness and new life?
- What did Jesus Christ do by dying on the cross? Did he actually and effectively satisfy the just wrath of the Father, or did he merely set an example of self-sacrifice for his followers?
- What happens when someone becomes a Christian?
- If we are Christians, can we be sure that God will continue to care for us? If so, is his continuing care based on our faithfulness or on his?

All these questions are not simply for bookish theologians or young seminary students. They are important for every Christian. Those of us who are pastors know how differently we would shepherd our people if our answer to any one of the above questions changed. Faithfulness to Scripture demands that we speak about these issues with clarity and authority, as does our desire to display the character of God in all its fullness.

Just consider: If we want churches that display God's character, don't we want to know everything he has revealed about himself in the Bible? What does it say about our opinion of his character if we don't?

RESISTING GOD'S SOVEREIGNTY

Our understanding of what the Bible teaches about God is crucial. The biblical God is Creator and Lord. Yet his sovereignty is sometimes denied, even within the church. When confessing Christians resist the idea of God's sovereignty in creation or salvation, they are really playing with pious paganism. Christians will have honest questions about God's sovereignty. But a sustained, tenacious denial of God's sovereignty should concern us. To baptize such a person may be to baptize a heart that remains, in some ways, unbelieving. To admit such a person into membership may be to treat the individual as if he or she were trusting God when in fact he or she's not.

Such resistance is dangerous in any Christian, but it's even more dangerous in the leader of a congregation. When a church appoints a leader who doubts God's sovereignty or who misunderstands the Bible's teaching, that church sets up as their example a person who may be deeply unwilling to trust God. And this is bound to hinder that church's growth.

Too often today, the consumer-driven and materialistic culture around us encourages churches to understand the Spirit's work in terms of marketing and to turn evangelism into advertising. God himself is made over in the image of man. In such times, a healthy church must be especially careful to pray that its leaders would have a biblical and an experiential grasp of God's sovereignty. They should also pray that their leaders would remain fully committed to sound doctrine in its full, biblical glory. A healthy church is marked by expository preaching and by theology that's biblical.

WEEK 1
WHAT IS SOUND DOCTRINE AND WHY DOES IT MATTER?

GETTING STARTED

Theology has gotten a bad rap lately. To some, the very word "theology" conjures up images of medieval monks in ivory towers musing over how many angels can stand on the head of a pin. Others think of sleep-inducing lectures. To others, it signifies an outdated way of thinking that simply doesn't work for postmodern people.

1. What are some objections to theology that you've heard? (Or said!)

The New Testament consistently places a strikingly high priority on theology and doctrine. According to the New Testament, sound doctrine—that is, teaching that conforms to God's Word—is of first importance for the Christian life and for the entire church.

MAIN IDEA

Sound doctrine is teaching that rightly explains what God has revealed to us in his Word. Sound doctrine is essential to the church and the Christian life because it is a central means by which we grow to maturity in Christ.

DIGGING IN

Throughout 1 Timothy, 2 Timothy, and Titus, the apostle Paul insists that sound doctrine is of first importance in the life of the church. Consider the following passages:

- 1 Timothy 1:3–5: [3] As I urged you when I was going to Macedonia, remain at Ephesus so that you may charge certain persons not to teach any different doctrine, [4] nor to devote themselves to myths and endless genealogies, which promote speculations rather than the stewardship from God that is by faith. [5] The aim of our charge is love that issues from a pure heart and a good conscience and a sincere faith."

- 1 Timothy 4:16: "Keep a close watch on yourself and on the teaching. Persist in this, for by so doing you will save both yourself and your hearers."
- 1 Timothy 6:2b–4a: "Teach and urge these things. [3] If anyone teaches a different doctrine and does not agree with the sound words of our Lord Jesus Christ and the teaching that accords with godliness, [4] he is puffed up with conceit and understands nothing."
- 2 Timothy 1:13–14: "Follow the pattern of the sound words that you have heard from me, in the faith and love that are in Christ Jesus. [14] By the Holy Spirit who dwells within us, guard the good deposit entrusted to you."
- 2 Timothy 2:15: "Do your best to present yourself to God as one approved, a worker who has no need to be ashamed, rightly handling the word of truth."
- Titus 1:9–11: "[An elder] must hold firm to the trustworthy word as taught, so that he may be able to give instruction in sound doctrine and also to rebuke those who contradict it. [10] For there are many who are insubordinate, empty talkers and deceivers, especially those of the circumcision party. [11] They must be silenced, since they are upsetting whole families by teaching for shameful gain what they ought not to teach."
- Titus 2:1: "But as for you, teach what accords with sound doctrine."

WHAT IS SOUND DOCTRINE?

Sound doctrine is the sum total of the Bible's teaching on any given topic.

In other words, sound doctrine is what we get when we consider what all of Scripture has to say about a given topic: the character of God, sin, salvation, the church, and so on. In the passages above, Paul's references to sound doctrine especially focus on the good news about Jesus Christ and how we are to live in light of that good news.

HOW DO WE GET SOUND DOCTRINE?

Think about what we do when we read different passages that explain God's character. First John 4:8 says that God is love. Yet in other passages we learn that God is just and holy and therefore that his wrath burns against sin (see Hab. 1:13).

So what do we do? Pick and choose the passages we like? Claim that if God is loving, then he would never punish people for their sin? Of course not. As Christians, we embrace all of what Scripture teaches about God, so we come to understand that God is both just and loving, both kind and severe, both holy and merciful. This developed, comprehensive picture of God's character is one aspect of sound doctrine.

1. Drawing on the seven passages listed before, fill in the chart below with characteristics *of sound doctrine (What is it? How does Paul describe it?) and* results *of sound doctrine (What follows when sound doctrine is taught? How does it impact our lives?). Also, list the verse each characteristic or result comes from.*

Characteristics of Sound Doctrine	Results of Sound Doctrine

2. Is there anything that surprised you about sound doctrine as you went through these passages?

3. Based on Paul's teaching in these passages, how would you respond to someone who said that sound doctrine is something that changes through time?

4. Based on these passages, how would you respond to someone who said that sound doctrine is an optional add-on for intellectual Christians who enjoy that sort of thing?

5. Based on these passages, would you say that Paul understands sound doctrine to be something purely intellectual? (See especially passages 1, 3, and 4.) Explain.

6. In the chart below, list the characteristics and results of false teaching (see especially passages 3 and 6).

Characteristics of False Teaching	Results of False Teaching

7. Is there anything that struck you or surprised you about false teaching?

8. Based on Paul's teaching in these passages, what are pastors supposed to do about false teaching? What should you do about false teaching?

9. Can you think of some examples of the practical consequences of abandoning sound doctrine? What might happen in our lives if we forsake the biblical doctrines of:

    a) The inspiration and authority of Scripture?
    b) Salvation by God's grace alone through faith alone in Christ alone?
    c) The sovereignty and goodness of God?

10. Why would you say that sound doctrine is important for:

    a) The corporate life of the church?
    b) How a pastor prepares a sermon or you prepare a Bible Study?
    c) Your growth as a Christian?

11. Name something you struggle with in the Christian life. What biblical doctrines can help you address this struggle? How can you practically seek to grow in understanding and applying sound doctrine as it relates to this area?

12. Can you think of a struggle that you've seen a church have, which was then addressed and remedied by sound doctrine?

WEEK 2
SOUND DOCTRINE IS FOR LOVE

GETTING STARTED

Does your church divide itself into "love people" and "doctrine people"?

The "love people" perceive themselves as all about the heart, while the "doctrine people" perceive themselves as being all about the mind. The "love people" are all about helping others, and the "doctrine people" are all about proclaiming the truth. Both sides say to the other, "What *we're* doing is what really matters."

Today, the "love people" are likely to speak loudest and win the biggest hearing. After all, who doesn't want love? More to the point, who wants a bunch of loveless, cold, dry, abstract ideas when you could have love instead? Does this sound familiar?

1. Why do you think people so often set love and doctrine against each other like this?

MAIN IDEA

In the church, sound doctrine is the basis for our love for one another, and love is the goal of sound doctrine.

DIGGING IN

John's second Epistle powerfully fuses together love and sound doctrine. It's a very short letter, so let's consider the whole thing:

> [1] The elder to the elect lady and her children, whom I love in truth, and not only I, but also all who know the truth, [2] because of the truth that abides in us and will be with us forever:

³ Grace, mercy, and peace will be with us, from God the Father and from Jesus Christ the Father's Son, in truth and love.

⁴ I rejoiced greatly to find some of your children walking in the truth, just as we were commanded by the Father. ⁵ And now I ask you, dear lady—not as though I were writing you a new commandment, but the one we have had from the beginning—that we love one another. ⁶ And this is love, that we walk according to his commandments; this is the commandment, just as you have heard from the beginning, so that you should walk in it. ⁷ For many deceivers have gone out into the world, those who do not confess the coming of Jesus Christ in the flesh. Such a one is the deceiver and the antichrist. ⁸ Watch yourselves, so that you may not lose what we have worked for, but may win a full reward. ⁹ Everyone who goes on ahead and does not abide in the teaching of Christ, does not have God. Whoever abides in the teaching has both the Father and the Son. ¹⁰ If anyone comes to you and does not bring this teaching, do not receive him into your house or give him any greeting, ¹¹ for whoever greets him takes part in his wicked works.

¹² Though I have much to write to you, I would rather not use paper and ink. Instead I hope to come to you and talk face to face, so that our joy may be complete.

¹³ The children of your elect sister greet you.

1. It's likely that "the elect lady and her children" in verse 1 is simply a way of referring to the entire local church John was writing to. Who, according to John, loves this local church? Why (vv. 1–2)?

2. What command does John give to the church in verses 5 and 6?

3. Who does John warn the church against in verses 7 through 11? How does he instruct the church to treat these individuals?

4. Notice that verse 7 starts with the word "for," which simply means "because." John is especially exhorting the church to love each other (vv. 4–6) because many false teachers are trying to deceive them with destructive doctrine (vv. 7–11). John evidently thought that the deceivers' false doctrine posed a serious threat to these Christians' love for each other if they came to embrace it.

How could false teaching undermine Christians' love for each other? (Hint: Consider what verses 1–2 teach us about the basis of Christians' love for each other.)

5. Based on John's teaching in this passage, how would you respond to someone who said, "What God cares about is not that we have right doctrine, but that we love others"?

Another passage that tightly ties together love and sound doctrine is Paul's opening exhortation to Timothy in 1 Timothy 1:3–5:

> [3] As I urged you when I was going to Macedonia, remain at Ephesus so that you may charge certain persons not to teach any different doctrine, [4] nor to devote themselves to myths and endless genealogies, which promote speculations rather than the stewardship [or *good order*] from God that is by faith. [5] The aim of our charge is love that issues from a pure heart and a good conscience and a sincere faith.

6. For what purpose does Paul tell Timothy to remain at Ephesus (v. 3)?

7. What practical consequences does this "different doctrine" lead to (v. 4)?

8. What is the goal of Paul's instruction to Timothy (v. 5)?

9. According to Paul, how do we grow in love? Is it simply an emotion we stir up in ourselves?

10. Based on Paul's teaching in this passage, how would you interact with someone who apparently loves to study theology (a "doctrine person") but whose life is not marked by consistent, sacrificial love for others?

It's clear that both "love people" and "doctrine people" are wrong if they think you can have one and simply ignore the other. Yet what we see in both of these passages is that sound doctrine is the foundation for love. It's what fuels and enables love, whether love for others or love for God. None of us *should* have sound doctrine without love, and none of us *can* truly have love without sound doctrine.

11. How has your love for God and others grown as a result of being taught sound doctrine? Give specific examples.

12. What would it look like to love someone who:

    a) Doesn't believe that Jesus is the only way to be saved?

    b) Is struggling to trust in God's sovereignty and goodness during a severe trial?

WEEK 3
SOUND DOCTRINE IS
FOR HOLINESS

GETTING STARTED

We live in an age of information overload. Emails, blogs, text messages, twenty-four-hour news, Twitter, and more all add up to vast amounts of information daily passing in front of our eyes.

1. What are some examples of information you regularly encounter that have little or no impact on your life?

2. What's one piece of information or one idea that radically changed your life?

In this study we're going to consider how one specific kind of information—sound doctrine—is intended by God to have a dramatic impact on our lives as Christians: namely, growing us in holiness.

MAIN IDEA

Sound doctrine is a central means by which Christians grow in holiness, and holiness is the goal of sound doctrine.

DIGGING IN

In John 17, Jesus prays for his disciples in view of his impending death and resurrection. After praying that God would keep them in his name, just as Jesus himself had kept them in God's name, he continues:

> ¹³But now I am coming to you, and these things I speak in the world, that they may have my joy fulfilled in themselves. ¹⁴ I have given them your word, and the world has hated them because they are not

of the world, just as I am not of the world. [15] I do not ask that you take them out of the world, but that you keep them from the evil one. [16] They are not of the world, just as I am not of the world. [17] Sanctify them in the truth; your word is truth. [18] As you sent me into the world, so I have sent them into the world. [19] And for their sake I consecrate myself, that they also may be sanctified in truth. (17:13–19)

1. According to verse 13, what is the goal of Jesus's prayer?

2. How does Jesus intend for this goal to come about (v. 13)?

3. What does Jesus ask the Father to do in verse 17?

To "sanctify" something means to set it apart or devote it to a specific purpose. For a person to be sanctified is for that person to be separated from sin and totally devoted to God's purposes. The Bible teaches that as Christians we *have been* sanctified (1 Cor. 6:11). That is, when we became Christians we were purified, given new natures, and set apart for God's service. It also teaches that we *are being* sanctified as we grow in overcoming sin and obeying God (1 Thess. 4:1–3).

4. What are some practical examples of what sanctification looks like in everyday life?

5. In verse 17, Jesus prays that the Father would sanctify us by his Word, which is truth. What are some ways in which people attempt to pursue holiness that ignore or bypass or minimize God's Word?

6. How would you apply sound doctrine to help someone grow in the following areas of life? What are some specific doctrines that are especially relevant to each of these?

    a) Faithfulness at work
    b) Discernment and purity in the use of TV, the internet, and other media
    c) Dealing with difficult people
    d) Addressing racist thoughts and attitudes

In 1 Timothy 1:8–11, Paul shows that life and doctrine are inseparable. He writes,

> [8] Now we know that the law is good, if one uses it lawfully, [9] understanding this, that the law is not laid down for the just but for the lawless and disobedient, for the ungodly and sinners, for the unholy and profane, for those who strike their fathers and mothers, for murderers, [10] the sexually immoral, men who practice homosexuality, enslavers, liars, perjurers, and whatever else is contrary to sound doctrine, [11] in accordance with the gospel of the glory of the blessed God with which I have been entrusted.

7. *In this passage Paul mentions a long list of immoral behaviors that appears to be a condensed summary of the Ten Commandments. What does he say that these immoral actions are contrary to (v. 10)?*

8. *What does the answer to the previous question teach us about sound doctrine?*

9. *In light of Paul's teaching in this passage and Jesus's prayer in John 17, how would you respond to someone who said, "What matters to God is that we live holy lives, not that we have good theology"?*

10. *How should this inseparable bond between sound doctrine and holy living inform a pastor's regular preaching?*

11. *A church's work of evangelism and missions should result from its growing love, but it should also result from its growing holiness. Do you see the connection between the call to holiness and the call to evangelize? What is it?*

12. *What are some ways that sound doctrine has equipped you personally to live a more holy life? Give specific examples.*

WEEK 4
SOUND DOCTRINE IS
FOR WORSHIP

GETTING STARTED

Sadly, worship is a battleground in many churches today. Skirmishes over volume, instrumentation, and style frequently divide churches. In all of these "worship wars," the focus is almost exclusively on music, and especially on the style of music.

1. Do you see any problems or dangers in investing so much in a specific style of music's use in the church?

Combatants in the worship wars may be surprised to learn that the Bible tells us very little about the style of music churches should sing. On one hand, the New Testament does provide a pattern for what kinds of activities churches should do in their corporate gatherings (namely, singing, praying, reading Scripture, preaching, and celebrating baptism and the Lord's Supper). On the other hand, it says little about matters of style. In fact, as Christians, Scripture tells us far more about *why* to worship God than about *how* to worship him.

Simply put, Scripture tells us that we are to worship God because of who he is and what he has done. In other words, worship is fueled by *sound doctrine*.

MAIN IDEA

Sound doctrine fuels our worship of God because true worship is praising God for who he is and what he has done.

DIGGING IN

Countless passages of Scripture call on God's people—and all people—to worship God for who he is and what he has done. This is a common theme throughout the Psalms, especially Psalm 96:

> ¹ Oh sing to the LORD a new song;
>   sing to the LORD, all the earth!
> ² Sing to the LORD, bless his name;
>   tell of his salvation from day to day.
> ³ Declare his glory among the nations,
>   his marvelous works among all the peoples!
> ⁴ For great is the LORD, and greatly to be praised;
>   he is to be feared above all gods.
> ⁵ For all the gods of the peoples are worthless idols,
>   but the LORD made the heavens.
> ⁶ Splendor and majesty are before him;
>   strength and beauty are in his sanctuary.
>
> ⁷ Ascribe to the LORD, O families of the peoples,
>   ascribe to the LORD glory and strength!
> ⁸ Ascribe to the LORD the glory due his name;
>   bring an offering, and come into his courts!
> ⁹ Worship the LORD in the splendor of holiness;
>   tremble before him, all the earth!
>
> ¹⁰ Say among the nations, "The LORD reigns!
>   Yes, the world is established; it shall never be moved;
>   he will judge the peoples with equity."
>
> ¹¹ Let the heavens be glad, and let the earth rejoice;
>   let the sea roar, and all that fills it;
>   ¹² let the field exult, and everything in it!
> Then shall all the trees of the forest sing for joy
>   ¹³ before the LORD, for he comes,
>   for he comes to judge the earth.
> He will judge the world in righteousness,
>   and the peoples in his faithfulness.

1. What does the psalmist command his hearers to do in verses 1 and 2a?

2. What does the psalmist command his hearers to do in verses 2b and 3?

3. In several places in this psalm, the author gives reasons why people should worship God and declare his greatness to others. List all of them in the form "We should praise God because _____." (Hint: Look for the word "for." This indicates that the author is giving a reason for his command to worship God.)

4. In verse 8, the psalmist invites us to "ascribe to the LORD the glory due his name." What does that mean? What does this verse teach us about worship?

5. What does the psalmist command us to declare to the nations and peoples? (See vv. 2–3, 10.)

6. How is telling others about God's glory, salvation, and sovereignty an act of worship?

7. As we've seen in this psalm, the heart of worship is giving glory to God for who he is and what he has done. How then does sound doctrine relate to worship?

8. Can we truly worship God without sound doctrine? Why or why not?

9. If sound doctrine is what fuels our worship, what kind of songs should churches sing?

10. Based on this psalm's teaching, how would you respond to someone who viewed worship as a purely emotional, ecstatic experience, something that's too deep for words?

11. In 1 Timothy 4:13 Paul commands Timothy, "Until I come, devote yourself to the public reading of Scripture, to exhortation, to teaching." In light of Psalm 96, explain why public Scripture reading in a church service is an appropriate act of worship. (Think especially about this psalm's link between singing to the Lord and declaring God's praise to others.)

12. Many Christians think of worship exclusively in terms of singing, so their churches have the "worship" time and then the sermon. In light of this psalm's teaching, how would you say preaching relates to worship? Is preaching, and listening to preaching, an act of worship?

13. How has your understanding of sound doctrine increased your love for God and your worship of God? Can you give specific examples of how your growth in the knowledge of God—even coming to understand specific doctrines—has led you to worship God more heartily and devotedly, and to declare his praise to others?

WEEK 5
SOUND DOCTRINE IS
FOR WITNESS

GETTING STARTED

1. Have you ever been in a situation where you had to speak publicly but really didn't know what you were talking about? If so, describe what happened. How did it turn out?

Sadly, that's exactly what evangelism often feels like for many of us. We shy away from sharing the gospel with others because we don't really know how to explain the gospel or how to answer the questions people may ask.

This common (and understandable!) feeling that many Christians have is one reason among many why sound doctrine is necessary for evangelism.

MAIN IDEA

Sound doctrine is necessary for evangelism because evangelism is: 1) telling others the truth about God, our sin, and what God has done in Christ to save sinners, and 2) calling them to repent of their sin and to trust in Christ.

DIGGING IN

Acts 17 records for us Paul's address to the Areopagus council in Athens. This passage is often cited as an example of how Christians should adapt the method of our evangelism to suit different cultural contexts, or how we should search for points of contact with non-Christians in order to share the gospel with them. But Paul didn't merely adapt his style or find points of contact with his hearers in Acts 17—he evangelized them by preaching sound doctrine.

When Paul was in Athens, he preached the gospel to anyone who happened to be in the marketplace (Acts 17:16–17). Eventually he was brought before the Areopagus, a council of leading Athenians, to explain the "strange teaching" that he was presenting. Acts 17:22–34 records a summary of Paul's speech and their response:

> [22] So Paul, standing in the midst of the Areopagus, said: "Men of Athens, I perceive that in every way you are very religious. [23] For as I passed along and observed the objects of your worship, I found also an altar with this inscription, 'To the unknown god.' What therefore you worship as unknown, this I proclaim to you. [24] The God who made the world and everything in it, being Lord of heaven and earth, does not live in temples made by man, [25] nor is he served by human hands, as though he needed anything, since he himself gives to all mankind life and breath and everything. [26] And he made from one man every nation of mankind to live on all the face of the earth, having determined allotted periods and the boundaries of their dwelling place, [27] that they should seek God, and perhaps feel their way toward him and find him. Yet he is actually not far from each one of us, [28] for
>
> "'In him we live and move and have our being';
>
> as even some of your own poets have said,
>
> "'For we are indeed his offspring.'
>
> [29] Being then God's offspring, we ought not to think that the divine being is like gold or silver or stone, an image formed by the art and imagination of man. [30] The times of ignorance God overlooked, but now he commands all people everywhere to repent, [31] because he has fixed a day on which he will judge the world in righteousness by a man whom he has appointed; and of this he has given assurance to all by raising him from the dead."
>
> [32] Now when they heard of the resurrection of the dead, some mocked. But others said, "We will hear you again about this." [33] So Paul went out from their midst. [34] But some men joined him and believed, among whom also were Dionysius the Areopagite and a woman named Damaris and others with them.

1. How does Paul address the Athenians' religious beliefs in this speech? What does he proclaim to the Athenians? (See v. 23 in particular.)

2. What are all the different biblical doctrines that Paul explains or refers to in this passage? See how many you can list in the chart below. (Hint: More or less the entire speech contains doctrinal content.)

Doctrine	Verse

3. How did Paul's teaching about God confront the Athenians' religious beliefs and practices? List specific examples. (Hint: Luke tells us that the city was full of idols [v. 16], and Paul mentions these idols made of gold and silver in verse 29.)

4. Look over your list of doctrines from this speech again. What are all the things Paul teaches about who God is and what he's done? Why did the Athenians need to understand these things in order to understand the gospel?

5. In verses 25 through 29, Paul focuses specifically on God's creation of man and our relationship to him. How would you summarize Paul's teaching in this section in your own words? List the different elements below.

6. Why was it important for the Athenians to understand all of these biblical teachings we discussed in question 5? Do you think they could understand the gospel apart from them?

7. In light of this passage, how would you respond to someone who said that studying doctrine is a waste of time, a distraction from the task of evangelism?

In this speech, Paul probably spent so much time unpacking the biblical teaching on God, creation, mankind, and judgment because the Athenians were ignorant of the Bible's teaching on these topics, and they held false beliefs which led them astray from worshiping the true God. In other words, the Athenians were biblically illiterate, as are many people in the West today.

8. What do you think are some of the most important lessons this passage gives us for evangelizing those who are unfamiliar with the Bible and its teachings?

Elsewhere in Acts, we read records of Paul's evangelistic addresses to Jews, who had an intimate knowledge of the Scriptures. In these addresses, Paul focuses on proving that Jesus is the Christ, the longed-for Messiah who fulfills all of God's promises to his people (see, for example, Acts 13:13–41). So, Paul took a slightly different approach to evangelizing those who knew the Bible and those who didn't, although the substance of Paul's preaching was always Jesus Christ and him crucified (1 Cor. 2:2).

9. What doctrines may be especially important to emphasize when you're evangelizing someone who is familiar with the Bible, and perhaps considers himself or herself to be a Christian, but has not truly repented of sin and trusted in Christ for salvation?

10. We've already seen that much of what Paul said was intended to directly confront the Athenians' false beliefs. What are some unbiblical beliefs that you often run into when you're sharing the gospel with others? What biblical doctrines are most helpful for addressing them?

11. Why should growing in our understanding of sound doctrine motivate us to evangelize more?

12. What are some ways that growing in your understanding of biblical doctrine has helped you to be a better evangelist?

WEEK 6
SOUND DOCTRINE IS
FOR UNITY

GETTING STARTED

"Doctrine divides." Those two words have recently become a manifesto among those who think that what really matters is Christian unity and that doctrine only gets in the way.

Those who say this have a point. Christians throughout the ages have drawn boundaries over doctrinal issues, including everything from the Trinity and the deity of Christ to such secondary issues as baptism and church government.

1. Which do you think is more important: unity or doctrine?

2. Do you think it's ever right for Christians to draw boundaries over doctrine? If so, when?

MAIN IDEA

Sound doctrine is the ground of and motivation for Christian unity, and unity is one of the goals of sound doctrine.

DIGGING IN

In Ephesians 4, Paul turns from expounding the riches of salvation in Christ to calling the Ephesian church to live in light of those truths:

> [1] I therefore, a prisoner for the Lord, urge you to walk in a manner worthy of the calling to which you have been called, [2] with all humility and gentleness, with patience, bearing with one another in love, [3] eager to maintain the unity of the Spirit in the bond of peace.

> [4] There is one body and one Spirit—just as you were called to the one hope that belongs to your call—[5] one Lord, one faith, one baptism, [6] one God and Father of all, who is over all and through all and in all. (4:1–6)

1. In verses one through three, Paul exhorts the Ephesians to walk in a manner worthy of their calling, and then he specifies several specific ways they are to do this. In one sentence or phrase, how would you summarize what Paul is calling the Ephesians to do?

2. What does Paul stress about the Christian faith in verses 4–6?

3. How does this unity of the faith encourage us to pursue unity with one another? (Hint: If you want, you can look back through the first three chapters of Ephesians and consider how the things Paul teaches there foster unity in the church.)

Philippians 2:1–11 contains an exhortation similar to the one we just considered:

> [1] So if there is any encouragement in Christ, any comfort from love, any participation in the Spirit, any affection and sympathy, [2] complete my joy by being of the same mind, having the same love, being in full accord and of one mind. [3] Do nothing from selfish ambition or conceit, but in humility count others more significant than yourselves. [4] Let each of you look not only to his own interests, but also to the interests of others. [5] Have this mind among yourselves, which is yours in Christ Jesus, [6] who, though he was in the form of God, did not count equality with God a thing to be grasped, [7] but emptied himself, by taking the form of a servant, being born in the likeness of men. [8] And being found in human form, he humbled himself by becoming obedient to the point of death, even death on a cross. [9] Therefore God has highly exalted him and bestowed on him the name that is above every name, [10] so that at the name of Jesus every knee should bow, in heaven and on earth and under the earth, [11] and every tongue confess that Jesus Christ is Lord, to the glory of God the Father.

4. What does Paul tell the Philippians to do in this passage (v. 2a)?

5. By what *means are the Philippians to do this (vv. 2b–5)?*

6. *What threats to unity does Paul address in this passage?*

7. *List everything that Paul says Jesus did in this passage (vv. 6–8).*

8. *What has God done in response (vv. 9–11)?*

9. *How does Paul's teaching about Jesus in verses 5–11 address our temptations of pride, rivalry, and conceit?*

10. *Conceit, rivalries, and the threat of division are all very practical problems. Would you characterize Paul's instruction about these matters as purely practical? Explain.*

11. *In light of Paul's teaching in these passages, how would you respond to someone who said, "Doctrine is what divides Christians from each other. What we really need is to pursue unity."*

12. *In light of Paul's teaching in these passages, how would you instruct someone who loves sound doctrine but consistently causes divisions within the local church?*

13. *The doctrinal unity we share with other members of our church spills into other areas of our corporate and individual lives. How does doctrinal unity help:*

   a) When church members counsel one another?
   b) When church members interact with one another's children?
   c) When church members encourage one another through trials?
   d) When church members keep one another accountable in fighting against sin?
   e) When . . . can you think of other areas?

TEACHER'S NOTES FOR WEEK 1

DIGGING IN

1. The completed chart should look something like this:

Characteristics of Sound Doctrine	Results of Sound Doctrine
It is teaching that accords with what the apostles themselves taught (1 Tim. 1:3–5).	It leads to love that flows from a pure conscience and a sincere faith (1 Tim. 1:5).
It is founded on the very words of Jesus Christ (1 Tim. 6:2–4).	It leads to salvation (1 Tim. 4:16).
It establishes a pattern of life that Christians are to follow (2 Tim. 1:13–14).	It leads to a life of faith and love (2 Tim. 1:13–14).
It is something that has been entrusted to believers that we are to guard and preserve (2 Tim. 1:13–14).	When pastors rightly teach sound doctrine, they are commended by God and have no need to be ashamed before him (2 Tim. 2:15).
It is the standard by which God evaluates church leaders (2 Tim. 2:15).	It silences false teaching and prevents the spiritual disaster that false teaching causes (Titus 1:11).
It may be opposed in the church, which is one reason why elders need to be skilled in teaching it (Titus 1:9–11).	
It is to set the standard and the agenda for what church leaders teach (Titus 2:1).	

2. Answers will vary.

3. An appropriate response would be something along the lines of, "According to Paul, sound doctrine is not something that changes over time. Rather, it is a settled deposit of truth that Christians are called to steadfastly preserve and defend. Passages 3 and 4 speak to this.

- In 1 Timothy 6:2b–4a, "If anyone teaches a different doctrine . . ." indicates that there is one standard of doctrine to which Christians must adhere.
- In 2 Timothy 1:13–14, "Follow the pattern of the sound words . . . guard the good deposit" indicates that Timothy was to follow and preserve the apostolic teaching, not wavering from it or changing it.

4. An appropriate response would be something like, "According to Paul, sound doctrine is not just a hobby for brainy Christians but is essential for all Christians. Why? Because it is bound up with our very salvation (1 Tim. 4:16), and it is a crucial means by which we grow in godliness (1 Tim. 6:2b–4a)."

5. No, Paul doesn't understand sound doctrine to be purely intellectual. Rather, he understands that sound doctrine has profound, radical, comprehensive implications for how we live as Christians (see especially 1 Tim. 6:2b–4a).

6. The completed chart should look something like this:

Characteristics of False Teaching	Results of False Teaching
It contradicts the apostles' teaching (1 Tim 1:3).	It promotes speculation rather than a life of love (1 Tim. 1:5).
It contradicts the words of Jesus (1 Tim. 6:3).	It puffs up its teachers and hearers with conceit (1 Tim. 6:4).
It results from a refusal to submit to God (Titus 1:10, "insubordinate").	It upsets whole families (Titus 1:11).
It consists of empty talk and deception (Titus 1:10).	It can be financially profitable for those who teach it (Titus 1:11).

7. Answers will vary.

8. Based on Paul's teaching in these passages, pastors should rebuke and silence those who teach false doctrine (1 Tim. 1:3; Titus 1:9, 11). They primarily do this through consistently proclaiming the truth, though sometimes personal rebuke and confrontation will be necessary, as will public teaching that addresses serious theological errors.

9. There are a number of valid answers to this question. Here are some possibilities:

   a) If we forsake **the inspiration and authority of Scripture** we will be at liberty to reject anything in the Bible that we don't like, or that our culture opposes. This could result in the loss of the gospel itself. When we reject the inspiration and authority of Scripture, we're free to believe whatever we want, and our sinful hearts will set themselves up in judgment of God's revelation, rather than submitting to it in faith.
   b) If we abandon **salvation by God's grace alone through faith alone in Christ alone**, we will no longer be preaching the true gospel, which has eternal consequences. In addition, if we no

longer depend on God's grace alone for salvation, we will begin to either become puffed up with pride (if we think that we're actually attaining salvation by our efforts) or sink into despair (because we realize that we never can).

c) If we abandon either **the sovereignty or the goodness of God**, we will be unable to handle trials. In order to trust in God through difficult times, we need to know that he is in control. How could it be any comfort to say that God "did his best" but he couldn't stop something painful from happening? Not only that, we need to know that God is good and that he causes all things to work together for good for us (Rom. 8:28), even trials (Heb. 12:5–11). We need to know that God is *good* so that we don't wrongly begin to think that some difficult experience coming into our life means that God does not love us.

10–12. Answers will vary.

TEACHER'S NOTES FOR WEEK 2

DIGGING IN

1. According to verse 1, John and all who love the truth love this local church because of the truth that they believe in common.

2. The new command John gives the church in verses 5 and 6 is to love one another, which means obeying God's commandments.

3. In verses 7 through 11 John warns against false teachers, namely, those who do not confess the coming of Jesus Christ in the flesh. John instructs the church to watch themselves in order to protect against this false teaching (v. 8), and to keep totally separate from all of these false teachers, including not welcoming them into their homes.

4. False teaching can undermine Christians' love for each other because the truth we share in common is the ground of, and reason for, our love for each other. If we depart from the truth, we depart from that which unites us in love. False teaching can also undermine Christians' love for each other because false teaching *always* eventually brings about ungodly living. That's why John warns the church not to partake in these false teachers' "wicked works": the false teaching itself is a wicked work and it inevitably leads to more wicked works.

5. An appropriate response would be something along the lines of, "It's impossible to separate doctrine and love like that. John teaches us that God cares deeply that we embrace right doctrine, in part because it is the basis and ground of our love for others. If we want to love others, the way to do that is to embrace right doctrine, which will lead to love. After all, it's right doctrine that teaches us *who we are* in the gospel, and *who God is,* and *who other people are*. It's right doctrine that teaches us *what Christ did for us*. And it's when we grasp all these things that the affections of our hearts can begin to burn both genuinely and rightly."

6. Paul tells Timothy to remain in Ephesus in order that he may charge certain persons not to teach any different doctrine (v. 3).

7. This "different doctrine" promotes speculation rather than a rightly ordered life (v. 4).

8. The goal of Paul's instruction is love: that is, that believers, through being built up in sound doctrine, would lead lives of love for God and love for others (v. 5).

9. According to Paul, love is something that is informed by truth and flows from a pure heart, a good conscience, and a sincere faith. So love is not merely an emotion we stir up in ourselves, although it certainly has emotional aspects. Rather, it is the product of truth worked deeply into every area of our mind and heart.

10. An appropriate interaction with such an individual would involve reminding them that the goal of sound doctrine is love, so that if they are not living a life of love they're missing the point of the sound doctrine which they claim to love.

11–12. Answers will vary.

TEACHER'S NOTES FOR WEEK 3

DIGGING IN

1. The goal of Jesus's prayer is that the disciples would have his joy fulfilled in themselves (v. 13).

2. Jesus intends for his disciples to have his joy fulfilled in them *through* the things he has spoken in the world, that is, through their acceptance of and obedience to all of his teaching, including this very prayer (v. 13).

3. In verse 17, Jesus asks the Father to sanctify the disciples in the truth.

4. In everyday life, sanctification involves obeying God, fighting against sin, studying God's Word and praying so as to grow in the knowledge of God, serving others in love, sacrificing oneself for the good of others, and seeking to bring glory to God in every area of life. Many more practical examples could be offered.

5. Answers will vary but may include:

- People attempt to pursue holiness by contemplation and mysticism.
- People attempt to pursue holiness purely through social activism.
- People attempt to pursue holiness through ritual-based sacramentalism.
- People attempt to pursue holiness through ecstatic, extraordinary experiences, and so on.

6. Answers will vary.

7. Paul says that these immoral behaviors are contrary to *sound doctrine* (v. 10).

8. The answer to the previous question teaches us that sound doctrine commands sound living. Sound doctrine teaches us how to live in a way that pleases God.

9. An appropriate response would be something like, "While it is certainly very important to God that we lead holy lives, one of the most important *means* by which God intends to grow us in holiness is sound doctrine. So we can't simply neglect sound doctrine and attempt to focus all our efforts

on living holy lives. Rather, we need to devote ourselves to learning sound doctrine for the purpose of growing in living lives that please God."

10. There are a number of appropriate answers, including:

- Pastors should regularly include both doctrinal teaching and practical application in their sermons.
- Pastors *shouldn't* focus on either doctrinal teaching or practical application to the exclusion of the other.
- Pastors should attempt to trace the connections between doctrine and life, to show *how* sound doctrine should equip us to live holy lives; and so on.

11. To be "sanctified" or made holy is to be set apart for God's purposes. God's purpose is for all people to know him, which is what a church seeks through its work of evangelism and missions. A church growing in holiness, therefore, is a church which desires for more and more people to be freed from the slavery of sin and welcomed into the inheritance of God's children. In other words, holiness is not only personal, it's corporate.

12. Answers will vary.

TEACHER'S NOTES FOR WEEK 4

DIGGING IN

1. In Ps. 96:1–2, the psalmist commands his hearers to sing to the Lord a new song (v. 1) and to bless his name (v. 2a). That is, he commands us to sing praises to God, to worship him in song.

2. In verses 2b through 3, the psalmist commands his hearers to tell of God's salvation from day to day (v. 2) and to declare his glory among the nations (v. 3). That is, he commands us to tell those outside the people of God about who God is and what he has done.

3. We should praise God because he is great and because he is above all so-called "gods" (v. 4). We should praise God because, unlike the worthless idols of the peoples, God is the one who created heaven and earth (v. 5). We should praise God because he is the righteous judge of all and because he is coming to establish his kingdom (vv. 11–13).

4. To "ascribe to the Lord the glory due his name" (v. 8) is to give God the praise that he is due because of who he is. This verse teaches us that one aspect of worship is praising God for who he is.

5. The psalmist commands us to declare to the nations God's salvation (v. 2: "Tell of his salvation from day to day."), God's glory and great works (v. 3: "Declare his glory among the nations, his marvelous works among all the peoples!"), and God's sovereignty (v. 10: "Say among the nations, 'The Lord reigns!'").

6. Telling others of God's salvation, glory, and sovereignty is an act of worship because in telling others about who God is and what he has done, we give glory to God. Making known the truth about God brings glory to God. It honors God in the sight of all people. This is one reason we should share the gospel with others: it brings glory to God.

7. Sound doctrine is the ground of worship. It gives us reasons to praise God. Sound doctrine is also the content of our worship. This psalm itself is a song of praise to God. Its invitations to worship are also worshipful declarations of the glory and greatness of God. The reasons the psalmist gives us to praise God should then inform the praises we offer to God.

8. We can't worship God without sound doctrine. If we do not have right beliefs about God, we cannot offer him the glory that is due to his name, because worship is our response to who God is and what he has done.

9. Because sound doctrine fuels our worship, churches should sing songs that are filled with sound doctrine. Churches should sing songs that are filled with biblical words, phrases, and concepts that glorify God for who he is and what he has done for us in Christ.

10. An appropriate response would be something like, "If worship is purely an emotional, ecstatic experience, how does it really give glory to God? According to this psalm, we are to glorify God for who he is and what he's done. This means that our minds should engage and spur on our hearts and emotions as we praise God for his greatness, glory, and mighty acts."

11. Public reading of Scripture is an appropriate act for the gathered church to engage in because:

- Telling the truth about God brings God glory.
- Since our worship is a response to who God is and what he's done, it's appropriate as a church to hear the truth about God from God's Word and then respond to it in song and prayer. After all, to read Scripture is to proclaim God's glory and his mighty works to all who are present.

12. Answers will vary, but they should include the basic idea that preaching fuels worship because it gives us reasons to worship God. Preaching drives and informs worship because it portrays the greatness, glory, and grace of God to the church. And preaching itself should be viewed as an act of worship because, as with reading Scripture, proclaiming the truth about God (and humbly receiving and submitting to that proclamation) glorifies and honors God.

13. Answers will vary.

TEACHER'S NOTES FOR WEEK 5

DIGGING IN

Special note about the passage: During the session, someone may ask the question whether Paul is really doing evangelism here, since he never clearly proclaims the message about Christ's atoning death and resurrection. It's not totally clear from Luke's summary of this speech whether Paul actually proclaimed the gospel—the good news about Jesus's sin-bearing death and resurrection, which satisfied God's wrath for all those who would turn from their sin and trust in him—or whether he intended to but was cut off because people scoffed at his teaching on the resurrection (see v. 32). Either way, this passage can serve as a useful example of evangelism for us because in it we see Paul explaining Christian beliefs to non-Christians with a view to proclaiming the message of the cross to them.

1. In this speech, Paul confronts the Athenians' false beliefs by proclaiming a number of biblical doctrines to them, even though he never explicitly refers to any biblical text. In this speech, Paul proclaims to the truth about the God whom the Athenians recognize to some degree, but about whom they have no real knowledge (v. 23).

2. The completed chart should look something like this:

Doctrine	Verse
The doctrine of God. This includes his lordship over all and his self-sufficiency.	(vv. 24–28, esp. vv. 24–25)
God's creation of the whole universe	(v. 24)
God's special creation of man and the unity of the human race	(v. 26)
God's providential rule over man and direction of all of history	(vv. 26–28)
Man's responsibility to rightly serve God	(vv. 29–30)
The resurrection of Jesus Christ	(v. 31)

God's final judgment of all people	(v. 31)
The lordship of Jesus Christ (implied in his resurrection and his role as judge of all)	(v. 31)

3. The Athenians were polytheistic idolaters (see vv. 16, 29). That is, they believed in many gods and tried to earn the gods' favor by setting up idols and offering sacrifices. That's why Paul emphasizes that there is *one* true God who is Lord of all (v. 24), that God doesn't *need* our gifts or sacrifices because he is sufficient in himself (v. 25), and that because we are God's own creatures, we should know that he is not like something *we* make (v. 29). In all of these ways, Paul was directly confronting the Athenians' religious beliefs and practices.

4. The Athenians needed to understand all these things because the gospel only makes sense if we understand that God is our Creator and Lord and that we are morally accountable to him for how we live. They also needed to understand that their current worship was mistaken and unacceptable to God, so that they would come to realize that they are alienated from him and thus in need of a savior.

5. A summary of verses 26–29 should contain the following:

- Humans received everything we have, including life itself, from God (vv. 25, 28).
- God created the human race (v. 26).
- Because all people descend from the original man God created, all humans alike are accountable to God (v. 26).
- God established the times and places of all nations so that men should seek after him (vv. 26–27).
- Because God created humanity, we are all accountable to worship him rightly (v. 29).

6. It was important for the Athenians to understand all of these things about man and his relationship to God because in order to understand the gospel, it is necessary to understand that:

- We are all accountable to God for what we do.
- All of us have turned from God and have not lived as he wanted us to.
- Because God is holy, he will judge all sin and punish sinners.

It's important to understand all of these things about man in relationship to God because before we will seek a savior, we must understand that we need saving! Before we will seek to be reconciled to God through Christ, we must understand that God's wrath is against us because of our sin.

7. An appropriate response would be something like, "Studying sound doctrine isn't a distraction from evangelism because sound doctrine is *necessary for* evangelism. Evangelism is telling others the truth about God, our sin, and what God has done in Christ to save sinners, and calling people to repent of sin and trust in Christ. Therefore, the better we understand what the Bible teaches about all these things, the better we'll be able to share them with others."

8. This passage demonstrates that when we're evangelizing those who don't know the Bible's teachings, we need make sure to communicate biblical truths about God, his creation of all, his lordship, our accountability to him, and God's judgment against our sin. We need to communicate all these things so that our listeners will be able to understand what we mean when we speak about Jesus's death on the cross offering us salvation. Rather than simply assuming that people who know little or nothing about the Bible know what we mean when we say something like, "Jesus died on the cross for our sins," we should back up a few steps and explain the Bible's basic teaching about God, our accountability to him, and his judgment against sin.

9. Answers will vary. One particularly important doctrine when evangelizing such a nominal Christian is the doctrine of the new birth, which teaches that all who have genuinely trusted in Christ have undergone a radical spiritual transformation and will necessarily live lives that demonstrate that change in love for God and others.

10. Answers will vary.

11. Growing in our understanding of sound doctrine should encourage us to evangelize for a number of reasons:

- We will better understand and be able to better articulate the gospel.
- We will be better able to engage non-Christians' beliefs and answer their questions about the gospel.
- The more we come to understand the wonder of God's grace, the depth of his love for us, the sufficiency of Christ's sacrifice on the cross, and the terrible judgment that non-Christians face, the more those very doctrines should stir up our hearts to share the gospel with others.

12. Answers will vary.

TEACHER'S NOTES FOR WEEK 6

DIGGING IN

1. A good summary of Paul's teaching in these verses is that Paul is calling the Ephesians to pursue and preserve the unity of the church (see especially v. 3).

2. In verses 4–6 Paul stresses the unity of the Christian faith, that there is only one true faith and that this unity of faith pervades every aspect of the faith.

3. This unity of the faith encourages us to pursue unity with each other because when we realize that we all share the same body, Spirit, hope, Lord, faith, baptism, and Father, we will recognize the depth and richness of all that we have in common. This will enable us to see our differences as the relatively minor matters they really are. It will also stir us up to preserve the unity we have in the church because it consists of such precious, eternally significant matters.

4. In this passage Paul tells the Philippians to complete his joy (v. 2).

5. Paul tells the Philippians to complete his joy by means of "being of the same mind, having the same love, being in full accord and of one mind" (v. 2), by doing nothing from rivalry or conceit, but in humility counting others better than themselves (v. 3), and by looking to the interests of others (v. 4). They are to do all this by living as those who have the mind of Christ (v. 5).

6. In this passage, Paul addresses rivalry and conceit as threats to the Philippians' unity.

7. In this passage Paul says that Jesus:

- Did not count equality with God as a thing to be grasped (v. 6).
- But instead made himself nothing, making himself a servant by becoming a man (v. 7).
- And he humbled himself by becoming obedient to God even unto death on a cross (v. 8).

8. In response, God has "highly exalted [Jesus] and bestowed on him the name that is above every name, so that at the name of Jesus every knee

should bow, in heaven and on earth and under the earth, and every tongue confess that Jesus Christ is Lord, to the glory of God the Father." (vv. 9–11).

9. Paul's teaching about Jesus in verses 5–11 addresses our temptations of pride, rivalry, and conceit by expounding the doctrines of Christ's incarnation, humiliation, death, resurrection, and exaltation. That is, in response to these threats to unity, Paul reminds us of how Jesus humbled himself and supremely served others in order to accomplish our salvation. This doctrinal exposition about who Christ is and what he's done reminds us about the greatness of our salvation and its great cost to Jesus Christ. Moreover, Paul is explicitly telling us to imitate what Christ did (v. 5). So when we see how Jesus humbled himself, we understand what God calls us to as Christians.

10. It would be a mistake to characterize Paul's response to these practical problems as purely practical. Paul does, of course, practically exhort the Philippians to pursue unity, but the way he does this is by preaching doctrine to them!

11. An appropriate response would be something like, "Christians certainly do divide over doctrine, sometimes rightly so and sometimes perhaps needlessly. But sound doctrine, far from being the cause of division, is actually the ground of our unity as Christians. Doctrine is what unites us as believers. The shared truths we confess bind us together in profound ways. Not only that, but as we see in Paul's teaching, sound doctrine is what motivates us, what spurs us on to humbly pursue unity with one another. If you take away sound doctrine, you take away what actually unites Christians and what motivates us to bear with each other in unity."

12. In light of these passages, you could exhort such individuals by reminding them that the doctrines they so fervently believe are what unite them to other Christians. Further, because our doctrine is *about* a Savior who humbled himself for our sake, we who believe this doctrine are compelled to follow his example. So we must humble ourselves for the sake of serving others and pursuing unity in the church.

13. Answers will vary.

PERSONAL NOTES

PERSONAL NOTES

PERSONAL NOTES

PERSONAL NOTES

PERSONAL NOTES

PERSONAL NOTES

9Marks

Building Healthy Churches

9Marks exists to equip church leaders with a biblical vision and practical resources for displaying God's glory to the nations through healthy churches.

To that end, we want to see churches characterized by these nine marks of health:

1 Expositional Preaching
2 Biblical Theology
3 A Biblical Understanding of the Gospel
4 A Biblical Understanding of Conversion
5 A Biblical Understanding of Evangelism
6 Biblical Church Membership
7 Biblical Church Discipline
8 Biblical Discipleship
9 Biblical Church Leadership

Find all our Crossway titles
and other resources at
www.9Marks.org

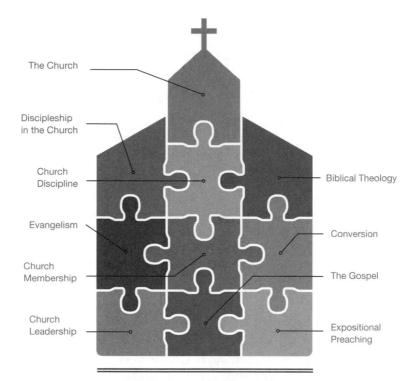

The Church
Discipleship in the Church
Church Discipline
Evangelism
Church Membership
Church Leadership
Biblical Theology
Conversion
The Gospel
Expositional Preaching

Be sure to check out the rest of the
9MARKS HEALTHY CHURCH STUDY GUIDE SERIES

This series covers the nine distinctives of a healthy church as originally laid out in *Nine Marks of a Healthy Church* by Mark Dever. Each book explores the biblical foundations of key aspects of the church, helping Christians to live out those realities as members of a local body. A perfect resource for use in Sunday school, church-wide studies, or small group contexts.